Siphon, Harbor

Siphon, Harbor

Brooklyn Copeland

Shearsman Books

First published in the United Kingdom in 2012 by
Shearsman Books
50 Westons Hill Drive
Emersons Green
Bristol
BS16 7DF

Shearsman Books Ltd Registered Office
30–31 St. James Place, Mangotsfield, Bristol BS16 9JB
(this address not for correspondence)

www.shearsman.com

ISBN 978-1-84861-202-0

Contents

My life
by water—
Hear

*

Tiered objects of her talking and water below.

*

what bursts in the very moment of bursting is image.

Homily

They had fished all night
but caught nothing.

        He implied that they would catch
in deep water.

                The command contained
a promise.
In reliance

on Your Word I will
        let down the nets.

Marina

Morse Lake forms
where the Big
creek meets

the Little creek—
        bits of boat,
        bits of dock

                mark the spot.

At the marina,
        we   skipped gravel
        to diseased
        ducks, wondering
if they'd mistake
        rocks for bread.

Hammers break open

geodes: scalene
jig-jags. My teeth

ache at the sound.

The hammers break, too.

Anonymous stinking fishes
        belly-up—
    mutable sequins glittering in the mud.
To this day, to me all
    silver smells red.

Someone's anemone
         unelaborate runtbud
muscling through
         woodwork

Termite trained to
grunt work
to false words

with white fists— my

sepal
quintuple.

People you know (your family

the unfettered
recovered in these:

your jaybird informant
informing instead
        a brochure sky

the heron
        nerd bird
        loner and long

the pelican
        as I recall him
        balding, indiscreet

seagulls at the sandfleas.

Unblemished flesh wasted

on the modest

(parse, mince, parse, mince)

the page's sincerest commands
sound us out; don't be scared

en plein jour
en plein air.

Nails and veins
teeth and skin

we can't know when
  incarnations

death disowns but life's
not ready:
spring

a choir somewhere's
singing *Hallelujah*

and they aren't just being ironic

and they aren't just hearing Jeff Buckley.

Homily

My kingdom is not   of this world is not
                    food and drink (because of this
            false idea the people

wanted to seize Him
and make Him

                    their breadking.   Beware lest you be misled

which was on everybody's mind because
they are so easily overcome by

            the false ideas of their age.

Bindweed

Sing-song
impulse   (no blood for melody
                    only rhythms only rustling

          knees sink and eyes—
shallow roots
          tendril about
                    fingers as if to
          claim
                    (anemic faces capsized
                              in the emergent

          glare—
rarely the science
so apparent

                    (weight of palms validates

lightning stabs laterally—

maybe rain
finally

Rain clarifies colors—

                    colors reveal the brief
ambition of these
             provincial weeds.
             In gullies,

        mosses soft, mosses bright

as dyed suede
feel rich beneath scrubbed feet.

        Rain— nature's iteration—

             light paradiddles
                    on the surface

                         of the creek.

How free-making this word
                   (penniless

before
a judge

Conversations
          braided
airtight   they pass,
                    wordless,
          between
gray-cast faces—

          stars caged by static
          (one jimmied free
soars, dissolves

: want to smell salt
but won't
                    water's vast
                    but fresh

cold sand
fanned upward
                    squeaks
underfoot

In some remote
pre-dawn eye slit

        the horizon largely
    the same

the cinquefoils still
chirpy and obliging the ox-eyed

      daisies and the daisies
           fleabane and the worts and weeds

      the thistles and yarrows
still healing and exotic
         in their ways—

weeds bind

tongues beard

thimbles berry

balms bee

flags blue

Bursts wrested   (endure, endure

>   your heart a horse's
as you breathe
uphill—

>   *culture*
>   was the whorl
>   of bees at the scent of fresh cut
>   wood

the calluses at the base
of your stained fingers

>   the at-first freedom
(the at-last burden

>   of god's
>   unhurried
precision

Nature remains
        faithful by
                natural light,
only. Immeasurable,
        invisible in the wind.
                Visible when
blades
        and branches bend.
                The wind
speaks fluent
        rain. Despite it
                the rain
falls straight. And beyond it
abandoned barns
                defend
        abandoned
men

Presque Vu

when low
down

        the bow
across
        the string
                stirred
        only fleas

in the grass

*

when blade slowed
to blade

floored the day

when few,

        stolen,
amassed,

flooded
to lots

*

when through
thin

walls
        voices fell—

hastened, fastened

      chastened

when blue-
      lidded silence

filled lines
where words
         sliced

*

         when white
birds were   signs,

never   symbols

Homily

obediently prepared the ark
although he could see no
signs

        obeyed to go
to a strange land although
he did not know
the story

before they slept together
they discovered
        He did not know
that this was in a dream

he did not sleep with her

Séance

In the bookish
teasoaked
         drowse

our own
séance.

*

Blue bone porcelain

white of unlit
         skin
yellow
         of skin
lit
         from within

stillness scaled
toward organic—

once is a twitch-
twice, a tic.

*

(dreamstream
      steamscene

the sun is milk bright

(twin rivulets
      cut the white

Symbol

Milled, folded
soldered.

Inlaid omen.
Mokume gane.

If as hinges.
Ands as pins.

Rings as
reunions.

Reservoir

the smallness of this
colloquial cannot

muffle the full morning orchestra—

amphibious greens
clotting the trickle

of thaw   the tinny

fin flip and eyeflake flash—
          small schools

giving shimmer in the dull

skulk of wind

(cry one
                pure perennial
                                I can't
doubt

(something by which to
                where we are
wearing our
belts

a little tighter

turbines' lull
on emptied road

rolls of fog burn clean

stillborn death of new

weather—
        failed western mother
        in awe

of herself

early dandelions

demand nothing
need only

        slow
nights—

awaken

to soft silver
            to blow

rotted out boat
bottom—
        the boat
will stay afloat

as long as you pretend to
                row

in meadows
let alone

gravid stems
erupt—

hale
yellows

gravid stems
erupt—

the hale
yellows pale once

they're plucked

Homily

"manifestation"
the word occurs six times

traditionally
Epiphany
was prophesied
hundreds of times

we do not know exactly
            what their relationship was
our testimony
should consistently

be the same
all the time

Symbol

Rings possess fingers.

Fingers remember
what the eyes have

blocked. The blindness
in this

case is figurative.
The figure in this

case is
curvaceous.

Rituals

Morning life
mewling robins

origami beaks
open

                    to receive
in the tangle

              just beyond the pane.

*   .

Two leaps
to depth—

          day prey
into water—

fat birds fed
        by hand.

Unceiled
vaporous
laughter—

she folds
her

red hands over

a pause—

       depth's triggered

in one supposed.

*

Her own psyche's burden
mid-hunt—

waste not,
want.

*

Her hair
   hennaed rust—

brush ends wet
with spit.

He made a slab
of soap slivers.
Same soap some years

later.
She could decipher

from his suds
the proof
    of space they shared—

dark hairs
near the drain—

tiny dark hairs.

Butter, caraway.

A tornadic dream with a tidy ending.

Ear to the linoleum
where it buckles.

Sky a clean-break blue.

Milk and rice for breakfast.

Sameness rinsed
of frankness.

Tiered objects of her talking

In any
pair
      one does—
      the other's
done   upon.

We   with our
rigorous allegiance
         to whim—

We   thrown
toward miscellany—

the loosened human
flakes—

any language
in which the verb
      to make is the same
as the verb
         to do

is the language
in which
         I write you—

warp to my weft.
Yawn I gallantly
swallowed.

Elbows fitted determinedly
(gaps in height, gait
we say

: the same
black bird seeing us back—

      his pylon orange epaulets
      dotting the bank's fog

: the sudden manmade scent—
pink cross between
amoxicillin and a gas leak
(childhood sidenotes   platonic ease

: the frog's guttural wooing—

           brutal umbrellic

humping,
thrashing.

: in our kiss, so much salt—

we taste we've broken
      a sweat.

With a beer
on the pier

you point to fish beds
but I can see
only swarms
                    of eels

boring themselves
            into   their meals.

Lightless night
yet noise
          crammed in by degrees
(cadences compete

          swell threateningly.

Hours layer
noise upon the moon.

We're attuned, if unskilled.

In any pair
one does as if doing's gracious—

       the other
as if sacrifice—

*

Any iridescence out here's
flimsy,

any sheen's unnatural.
The organic's matte—

the matte's most worthy

of trust, remark.

Any language
in which the verb
        to make is the same
as the verb
            to do

is the language
in which

            I allow you—

as if in this language
even the bible's true.

We allow the staff its flowers,

the whale his
appetite.

Homily

harbored earthly ideas

quiet the heart
          make the frightened

courageous—

Loss/Prevention

Furthest from
themselves

shelves of wild
                    flowers
           (eye   level
having
           climbed

faces jammed
& scentless
save

for some generic *green*—
petals
chewed in the process

                    of silvering
           the strip.

Hunger
        is young deer

galloping breakneck

to these failed
lilacs.

In your pocket

a knife, lighter.
mints tinful. A bowl.

            Clouds gain till
       fat rain's forfeited
over the neighbors,

we watch the radar, goslings
wade.

We scan the warmer pools

for crawdads.
We find

a massacre—

colorless husks jostled about—

a few, alive
confused.

(for Danielle)

Embedded
in the stream

the rocks' fur
sways, collects.

Insects skate
the surface.

Rust, rot
spread,
       tint.

Homily

Gospels are not biographies
but they do tell us enough

to know without his own

knowledge, the conditions,
the providence

that He would be born

that He would be called.

Seall

The dock spider's
quick work's
first preserved

by one admiring
man (himself
admired),
then

obliterated by
wind.

Wood
weathered
gray to bone
white feels

wetter
        than this
lapsed lake—

the johnboat's modest
wake stirs only
        frayed
weeds.

Our pulses
        gulp
        in rhyme
                upon
        release— our

bodies beyond
        us
        siphon,
                harbor.

Into smooth
common rocks
     spiraled fossils
          etched—
your blue eyes
wide set

& hair a naked
thicket crowded
     by red
cardinals (hands two frantic
brown ones

     & a back of moles
     and shoulders
     marred
by bites.

Laked,
        fielded,
                blanked.
                To the naked
eye too high
too wet
to give
            off color. Shaded
movement reveals
your sullen instinct
                to sink
too deep
before remembering to

reach. In days between touch
                        I remember you
not of, but as

duality—
            rurally surviving a city.

Border strand
        (grab-bag flora—

grayed seeds
            carried on
slinks of worm

drunken bees

duckfeet.

11:39AM, Grand Haven

Summer
seems lessened—

buds of cup-
      and-saucer scale
      to frayed
           extent.

Watching us

       the gull can
limn from

the edible
the purely

      ornamental.

The slow yellow
        sun hones
high wisps
from low threats—

planes
of a charged hour
bearing down

        on our
wet heads.

Parched beach grass
          holds the dune—

eleven lasts
          all morning.
No meaning

to assign yet
          to alewives
laid eerily by
                    the tide
two-by-two

                or your eyes
as you stare,
hardened to

(not the blue
                of the Lake
nor the blue
of the sky

                but the blue
                of a gray
rock

worn
memento smooth.

Through
bowlful redcurrant

breakfasts
      I will recall this
           minute—

steered to its brink
then
      sank.

Notes

The epigraphs are from Lorine Niedecker ('My Life by Water'), Michael Palmer ('Notes for Echo Lake 10'), and Gustaf Sobin ('On the Nature of the Iconic'), respectively.

The homilies are erasures from *The Sermon Notes of Dr. Harold Buls* [1920–1997]: *On the Gospel Lessons of the Ingrian Church Of Russia*, converted to ASCII for Project Wittenberg by Cindy A. Beesley; they are in the public domain.

Bodies addressed directly in these poems include Morse Reservoir in Hamilton County, Indiana ('Marina; Reservoir'), Long Lake in St. Joseph County, Michigan ('Tiered objects of her talking; Seall'), the White River on the north side of Indianapolis ('Loss/ Prevention'), and Lake Michigan in Grand Haven, Michigan ('11:39AM, Grand Haven').

Acknowledgements

Because he shares my lusts, reluctances, and watery horoscopes, these poems are for Mike Seall.

My gratitude goes to the editors of the following, where many of these poems first appeared, sometimes in slightly different versions: Blue Hour Press, Alice Blue Books, Spooky Girlfriend Press, Small Fires Press, Ungovernable Press, Little Red Leaves/ Textiles Series, and *Turntable & Blue Light, Sous Rature, Interrupture, Parcel, Burnside Review, Diode, Sink Review,* and *Poetry.*

With thanks especially to the following writer-types: Amber Nelson, Niina Pollari, Drew Kunz, Freke Räihä, Justin Runge, Kate Lorenz and Steven Karl.

& to Cortney Ellen-Settle Johnson for her generous and inspiring company.
& to the good people at the Poetry Foundation for their early and ongoing support.
& to my family (parents, siblings, and Sealls) for living fully and perfectly with me in the present tense.